ISBN 978-0-243-40204-5
PIBN 10795749

1 MONTH OF
FREE
READING

at
www.ForgottenBooks.com

By purchasing this book you are eligible for one month membership to ForgottenBooks.com, giving you unlimited access to our entire collection of over 700,000 titles via our web site and mobile apps.

To claim your free month visit:

www.forgottenbooks.com/free795749

English
Français
Deutsche
Italiano
Español
Português

www.forgottenbooks.com

Mythology Photography **Fiction**
Fishing Christianity **Art** Cooking
Essays Buddhism Freemasonry
Medicine **Biology** Music **Ancient**
Egypt Evolution Carpentry Physics
Dance Geology **Mathematics** Fitness
Shakespeare **Folklore** Yoga Marketing
Confidence Immortality Biographies
Poetry **Psychology** Witchcraft
Electronics Chemistry History **Law**
Accounting **Philosophy** Anthropology
Alchemy Drama Quantum Mechanics
Atheism Sexual Health **Ancient History**
Entrepreneurship Languages Sport
Paleontology Needlework Islam
Metaphysics Investment Archaeology
Parenting Statistics Criminology
Motivational

THE
BIBLE
VISION

*35th Anniversary of
the Bible Institute
MARCH 21ST*

MARCH - 1939

THE
FORT WAYNE
BIBLE
INSTITUTE

EST.   1904

PUBLISHED AT BERNE, INDIANA

By the FORT WAYNE BIBLE INSTITUTE
Fort Wayne, Indiana

THE BIBLE VISION

A Monthly Journal Reflecting the Light
of the Bible on Us and Our Times

Volume III	March, 1939	Number 6

Published monthly at Berne, Ind., by

THE FORT WAYNE BIBLE INSTITUTE

S. A. WITMER, *Editor* B. F. LEIGHTNER, *Ass't Editor*

LOYAL RINGENBERG, *Circulation Manager*

ELDA GERBER, *Editor of Fellowship Circle*

IRMA JUDD, *Institute News*

JOHN GREENFIELD, *Contributing Editor*

A. W. TOZER, *Contributing Editor*

ECONOMY PRINTING CONCERN, Berne, Indiana *Publisher*

Yearly Subscription, Seventy-Five Cents; Sixteen Months for One Dollar; Three Years for Two Dollars; Single Copy for Ten Cents.

Address all correspondence regarding subscriptions or subject-matter to The Bible Vision, Berne, Ind., or to the Fort Wayne Bible Institute, Fort Wayne, Indiana.

Entered as second class mail matter at the post office at Berne, Indiana, under the Act of March 3, 1879.

ARE YOU A NEW READER OF THE BIBLE VISION?

If so, and you haven't subscribed, we should like you to read this issue and consider becoming a regular reader. The Bible Vision is not a pretentious magazine as you may observe, but it does have some features that you will enjoy.

First, *it has a message.* It carries articles by capable writers which focus the light of the Bible on us and our times.

Second, *it is alive with reports of Christian action* in many parts of the world.

Third, *it is an instrument of fellowship and communication* among friends and patrons of the Fort Wayne Bible Institute. What are its graduates doing? What is taking place at the Institute? These are questions that the Bible Vision seeks to answer among a growing circle of friends.

Subscribe NOW. The rate is only 75c per year, $1.00 for 16 months, or $2.00 for three years. Send subscriptions to THE BIBLE VISION, BIBLE INSTITUTE, FORT WAYNE, INDIANA.

Editorially ---

PRAYING FOR THE POPE

To a Bible Christian it seems absurd that the soul of the late Pope should be the object of prayerful petitions from millions of lips. It reflects on his Christian integrity and his purported piety. To pray for the welfare of his soul makes the title "His Holiness" a misnomer. As the "Vicar of Christ on earth" he must have been an unworthy person to occupy such an exalted office.

When Catholics pray for their departed Pope we merely conclude that such is Roman Catholicism. But what shall we say when Protestants (?) mimic the deluded followers of Rome and join with them in prayers for the dead? In our city a minister of a leading Protestant (?) church asked his congregation to rise for a few moments of meditative silence and prayer for the repose of the Pope's soul! And we have learned since that quite a number of ministers throughout the country did likewise.

What shall we say? Words fail to express the contempt that we share for such disloyalty to Protestant principles and the apparent silly attempt to pattern after Rome. A Protestant is a *protester*—at least he is supposed to be. But many today in Protestant communions dislike the term. It smacks too much of intolerance! It is popular now to be tolerant, and the most that can be said for a good many "ministers" today is that they are time-serving, spineless, convictionless men who are for everything but against nothing. Of such our Lord will say in the day of His coming: "So then because thou art lukewarm, and neither cold nor hot, I will spue thee out of my mouth."

Rome hasn't changed one whit. She is on the march—while Protestants are asleep!

Praying for Current Needs

Rather than praying for the soul of the deceased Pope, Christians might well give themselves to a ministry of intercession which is the imperative need of the hour. The following current needs should challenge every one who bears the name of Christ:

1. For a mighty revival of spiritual life in the church.
2. For the unoccupied regions of the earth—Central Asia, Central Africa, etc.
3. For the whole Mohammedan block of 250,000,000 souls that constitutes a formidable wall of granite resistance to the advance of the Gospel. Under the caption of "Flashes From the Mission Front" this issue of the Bible Vision presents some appalling facts concerning certain areas in the Near East, which we hope will be read by all.
4. For God's purpose to be wrought out in China's crisis.
5. For grace and power to the oppressed Christians in many lands.
6. For missionaries.
7. For the return of Jesus Christ.

What Christ Means to The World

Dr. E. J. Bulgin

(Prize-winning essay given on Missionary Hour over WOWO, Fort Wayne, Indiana, Feb. 19. Dr. Bulgin received the first prize of $500.00 from Mr. Roger T. Babson for the best essay on the above subject.)

When you see a projectile flying through the air you do not need to be told that it was put in motion by some propelling force. From the size of the projectile, together with its weight, velocity and the distance it had travelled, you may safely infer something concerning the nature of the propelling force.

The thing that we see in motion resulting from the life of Jesus of Nazareth bears testimony to a force and intelligence more than human.

Men have made lasting impressions upon the world by founding empires, discovering scientific principles, leading victorious armies, contributing valuable things to literature, wisely administering important offices in church and state.

Jesus of Nazareth never founded an empire; never wrote a book; announced no new principle in nature; never led an army. No artist painted His portrait; no sculptor chiseled His features. He lived His simple life in a territory fifty by one hundred miles, and never left that territory except once when He went to Egypt, a babe in His mother's arms. He was born in a manger, lived for thirty years in obscurity, probably engaged in hard labor at a carpenter's bench.

At the age of about thirty-three He was condemned to death as a blasphemer of God and a traitor to Rome, and was accordingly crucified.

By three years of public life in a little corner of the world He made such an impression that after nineteen hundred years the leading nations of the world count time from His birth and four continents cease from their ordinary occupations to celebrate His birthday.

He entrusted to a little band of obscure men a joyful message to the world, and where that message has been proclaimed women are honored and little children are happier.

Jesus challenged the attention of the world by His many-sidedness. He meets the needs of all classes and conditions of men. As deep answereth deep, so He responds to the movings of each soul of man.

Call the roll of the world's workers and ask, "What Think Ye of Christ?" Their answers amaze us by their revelation of this many-sidedness of our Lord.

To the artist, He is the One Altogether Lovely
To the architect, He is the Chief Cornerstone
To the astronomer, He is the Sun of Righteousness, the Bright and Morning Star
To the agriculturist, He is the Sower of the Good Seed
To the angler, He is the Fisher of Men
To the baker, He is the Living Bread
To the biologist, He is the Life
To the builder, He is the Sure Foundation
To the bookkeeper, He is the Faithful Scribe
To the capitalist, Unsearchable Riches

To the carpenter, He is the Door
To the Christian, He is the Son of the Living God
To the disconsolate, He is the Comforter
To the drifting, He is an Anchor
To the doctor, He is the Great Physician
To the educator, He is the Great Teacher
To the farmer, He is the Sower, and the Lord of the Harvest
To the friendless, He is the Close-Sticking Friend
To the florist, He is the Rose of Sharon and the Lily of the Valley
To the geologist, He is the Rock of Ages
To the genealogist, He is the Name above every Name
To the guilty, a Propitiation
To the horticulturist, He is the True Vine
To the heavy-laden, He is the Burden-Bearer
To the hopeful, He is the Prophet of a New Day
To the judge, He is the Righteous Judge, the Judge of All Men
To the juror, He is the Faithful and True Witness
To the jeweler, He is the Pearl of Great Price
To the lawyer, He is the Counselor, the Lawgiver, the Advocate
To the secret lodge, He is the Only Password
To the lonesome, He is the Ever-Present Companion
To the lonely maiden, her Betrothed
To the mariner, He is the Great Polar Star
To the mother, He is the Loving Son
To the newspaper man, He is the Good Tidings of Great Joy
To the needy, He is the Source of Supply
To the oculist, He is the Light of the Eyes
To the philanthropist, He is the Unspeakable Gift
To the philosopher, He is the Wisdom of God
To the photographer, He is a Perfect Likeness
To the preacher, He is the Word of God
To the potter, Vessel of Honor
To the pilgrim, He is the Way
To the polluted, He is the Purger of Conscience
To the railroad man, He is the New and Living Way
To the sculptor, He is the Living Stone
To the student, He is the Incarnate Truth
To the sinner, He is the Lamb of God which taketh away the sin of
    the world
To the theologian, He is the Author and Finisher of our faith.
The theologian must answer this question—If this man of Galilee is
f this and has done all of this, why, after two thousand years, is it
have barely scratched the back of this old sin-cursed world?
The greatest handicap the Church has ever had is the unfaithfulness
s own members; galvanized, white-washed, veneered professors and
possessors have held back the triumph of the Church for the last two
sand years. In the first place we are pleasure mad, in the second
e the world is money mad, and in the theological realm we have hu-
ized God, we've deified man and we have minimized sin, and today·
Church has so compromised with the world, the flesh, and the devil

(Continued on page 8)

Eat and Live

REV. JOHN GREENFIELD, D.D.

Moravian Evangelist, Daytona Beach, Fla.

"Then Jesus said unto them, Verily, verily, I say unto you, Except ye eat the flesh of the Son of man, and drink his blood, ye have no life in you.

Whoso eateth my flesh, and drinketh my blood, hath eternal life; and I will raise him up at the last day.

For my flesh is meat indeed, and my blood is drink indeed.

He that eateth my flesh and drinketh my blood, dwelleth in me, and I in him.

As the living Father hath sent me, and I live by the Father; so he that eateth me, even he shall live by me."—John 6:53-57.

In 1825 a French scientist, Brillat Savarin, made the following announcement: *"Tell me what you eat, and I will tell you what you are."* Twenty-five years later a German scholar, Ludwig Feuerbach, issued a still stronger statement: "Man is what he eats."

In recent years modern science has confirmed the truth of both above declarations. The discovery of the so-called "Vitamin," the life elements of all foods, makes it clear that in the physical realm at any rate, *"we are what we eat."* But this natural law holds good also in the spiritual world. No words of Jesus were ever clearer and more emphatic than the words of our text. In these five verses the Master tells us in the plainest and most positive language no less than five times that all spiritual life and growth and power and service depend upon the spiritual food of which we partake. In other words, "It is all in the eating," and "WE ARE WHAT WE EAT."

Eat and Live

In the first recorded sermon of Jesus we are told, "Ye must be born again." It is therefore scriptural truth when we sing (John 3:7)

"Ye must be born again,
For so hath God decreed;
No reformation will suffice,
'Tis life poor sinners need."

But how may this life be obtained? Jesus tells us in the text: *"He that eateth my flesh and drinketh my blood, hath eternal life."* He makes it doubly strong by declaring: "Except ye eat the flesh of the Son of man and drink His blood, ye have no life in you." But what do these words mean? We are almost tempted to say with the Jews: *"How can this man give us his flesh to eat?"* John 6:52. Of course it is no material eating and drinking of which Jesus here speaks.

He explains this very clearly in the words: "It is the Spirit that quickeneth; the flesh profiteth nothing." John 6:53. But how and when does Jesus give us His flesh to eat and His blood to drink? We answer: *At the Cross.* Here it was that He gave His flesh for the life of the world. Here it is that we may spiritually eat His flesh and drink His blood. Eating is an art that need not be learned. Instinctively the little infant knows how to eat when brought into contact with its natural supply of food. So it is with the sinner. Place before him the bleeding, dying

Lamb of God and his soul begins to "eat and live."

That it is a spiritual eating and drinking on the part of the human soul we learn also from the words of the prophet: "Ho, every one that thirsteth, come ye to the waters; and he that hath no money, come ye, buy and eat." "Eat ye that which is good, and LET YOUR SOUL DE-LIGHT itself IN FATNESS. Incline your ear and come unto me; hear, and *your soul shall live.*" Isaiah 55:1-3.

One of the greatest soul winners of modern times, Mrs. Catherine Booth, "Mother of the Salvation Army," has truly said: "Do not tell any-body they are saved. I never do. I leave that for the Holy Ghost to do. I tell them how to get saved. I try to help them to the way of faith. I WILL BRING THEM UP AS CLOSE AS EVER I CAN TO THE BLESS-ED BROKEN BODY OF THE LORD, and I will try to show them how willing He is to receive them, and I know that when really they do RECEIVE HIM, the Spirit of God will tell them quickly enough that they are saved." Let every minister, Sunday School teacher and would-be soul winner deeply ponder the above words, especially the sentence, *"I will bring them up as close as ever I can to the blessed broken body of the Lord."* That is where and when and how the soul begins to eat and live. In the Garden God issued the fearful warning: "In the day thou eatest thereof," (the forbidden fruit) "thou shalt surely die." Gen-esis 2:17. But at the Cross God gives us His flesh to eat and the most certain promise that "In the day thou eatest thereof thou shalt surely live."

Nearly two centuries ago Sir Walter Shirley put this everlasting Gospel into song in the well-known lines:
"Sweet the moments, rich in blessing,
Which before the Cross I spend:
Life and *Health* and *Peace* possessing
From the sinner's dying Friend."

Eating and Abiding

Again and again the Saviour exhorted His disciples to abide in Him. "As the branch cannot bear fruit of itself, except it abide in the vine, no more can ye, except ye abide in me." John 15:4. At the same time He uttered the solemn warning: "If a man abide not in Me, he is cast forth as a branch, and is withered; and men gather them, and cast them into the fire and they are burned." John 15:6. The beloved disciple, who wrote this Gospel, repeated the exhortation in one of his last letters, written when nearly one hundred years of age: "And now, little chil-dren, ABIDE IN HIM; that when he shall appear, we may have con-fidence, and not be ashamed before him, at his coming." John 2:28.

Would we escape the doom of condemnation and the fate of becom-ing *"withered branches"*? We must "abide in Him." Would we have *"boldness"* and not be "ashamed before Him at His coming"? WE must "abide in Him." But how may we abide in Him? What must we do to "abide in Him"? Again, "it is all in the eating." Jesus tells us in our text: *"He that eateth my flesh and drinketh my blood, dwelleth, abideth, in me."* Our dwelling place must be at the Cross of Jesus. Here we feed upon the Lamb, as the Israelites of old, while they were trusting in the blood which they could not see. Here, at the Cross, "beholding the Lamb of God bearing the sin of the world," our souls *"eat his flesh and drink his blood."* Thus we dwell and abide in Him. What a safe dwelling place to abide in Christ! St. Paul said, "There is no condemnation to those who are in Christ," who dwell and abide in Christ. Romans 8:1. Daily coming to the Cross, daily eating His flesh and drinking His blood, they dwell—and abide in Him. No wonder the great American hymn-writer, Fanny Crosby, prayed,

> "Near the Cross! O Lamb of God,
> Bring its scenes before me;
> Help me walk from day to day,
> With its shadow o'er me!"

> "Near the Cross I'll watch and wait
> Hoping, trusting ever;
> Till I reach the golden strand
> Just beyond the river."

(To be continued)

WHAT CHRIST MEANS TO THE WORLD
(Continued from page 5)

that she has lost her testimony. We have too much church-anity and not enough Christianity—a cold, formal ritualism is the substitute for the old-fashioned, warmhearted Christ and Christianity.

Unless we can get an old-fashioned John Wesley, Charles Finney, Dwight L. Moody, Holy Ghost revival, the Chuich will have to shut up shop, close her doors and quit business. She is not reaching the world today and you know it. One of three things must happen and that mighty soon—first, an old-fashioned revival which will inject a saving influence into the conditions of modern society; or second, the coming of our Lord Jesus Christ; or third, we'll be on the rocks and a crash in our present democracy. We proud, boasting Americans will learn that our democracy is not a safe form of government until the people of that democracy become a safe people. *Nations that forget God perish from the earth* can be proven from the pages of history.

Wherever His name is known, and nowhere else, there are hospitals for the sick, homes for the orphans, asylums for the blind, and schools for the young of all classes.

Through faith in His name we see thousands of lives transformed. Drunkards are made sober; liars are made truthful; thieves are made honest; hypocrites made sincere; hard hearts are made tender; hatred is changed to love; cruelty to sympathy; avarice to liberality; selfishness to self-forgetfulness.

No mere man in history has or could have exerted so deep and lasting impressions. Only a super-man could, from His little corner, have put into operation such great and lasting forces for good.

Jesus of Nazareth, two thousand years ago, by His nail-pierced hands cut new channels in human history, changed the almanac of the world and swung the gates of empires off their hinges—and made the greatest nations of the world celebrate His birthday.

And He stands today the holiest among the holy, He is the mightiest among the mighty. And your eternal destiny depends upon this—your answer to this question—What Think Ye of Christ?—*Copyrighted and used by permission.*

How I Learned to Put My Trust in God

(A manuscript written by a student for an assignment in English IV)

What does that mean? Why, Abraham did that; he dared to believe God. It seemed an impossibility at his age that Abraham should become the father of a child; it looked incredible, and yet God called him a "father of many nations" before there was a sign of a child; and Abraham called himself "father" because God called him that. That is faith. ·It is to believe and assert what God says. "Faith steps on a seeming void, and finds the rock beneath."

Only say you have what God says you have, and He will make good to you all you believe. Only it must be real faith. All there is in you must go over in that act of faith to God.

One must be willing to live by believing and neither think nor desire to live in any other way. Be willing to see every outward light extinguished, to see the eclipse of every star in the blue heavens, leaving nothing but darkness and perils around, if God will only leave in your soul the inner radiance—the pure, bright lamp which faith has kindled.

The moment did come when I had to get off the ground of distrust, out of the nest of seeming safety, and on the wings of faith—just such a time as comes to the bird when it must begin to try the air. At times it seems as if I must drop to the earth; so it may seem to the fledgling. It, too, may feel very much like falling, but it does not fall; its pinions give it support, or, if they fail, the parent bird sweeps under and bears it upon its wings. Even so will God bear me if I trust Him.

"Well, but," you say, "did you cast yourself upon nothing?" That is what the bird seems to have to do. But we know that the air is there. And the air is not as unsubstantial as it seems. And I have learned that the promises of God are there. And they are not unsubstantial at all. I have learned that I can take Him at His word and trust Him, day and night.—Roy Johnson.

EPISTLE TO THE ROMANS

Chrysostom had it read to him once each week.

Melancthon copied it twice with his own hand, in order to become better acquainted with it.

Luther called it the chief book of the New Testament, and the perfect Gospel.

Coleridge regarded it as the profoundest book in existence.

Sir William Ramsey referred to it as the philosophy of history.

Godet spoke of it as the cathedral of Christian faith.

Dr. David Bacon said that the faith of Christendom in its best periods has been indebted to this epistle more than to any other portion of the Living Oracles.

Dr. W. H. Griffith Thomas asserted that a thorough study of Romans is a theological education in itself. He also said that a Christian life nourished in the Epistle of Romans would never lack the three great requisites of clear perception, strong conviction and definite usefulness.

—Selected.

Deep Thoughts on Great Themes
By REV. FREDERICK RADER, *New Brighton, Pa.*

In the year that King Uzziah died, I saw also the Lord, etc.—Isa. 6:1-8.

This vision is fraught with lessons of permanent instruction; it teaches clearly the method by which a sinner is saved from his sins and fitted for life's mission.

I. REVELATION—OBSERVATION
"I saw the Lord."
1. *His supreme authority*—sitting upon a throne, high and lifted up. Israel's king is dead, but the King of Israel lives.
2. *His magnificent aspect*—"His train filled the temple." An illusion to the flowing robes of oriental monarchs which signalizes their stately grandeur. "Thou clothest thyself with light as with a garment."
3. *His illustrious attendants*—"Above it stood the seraphim." Eastern monarchs had numerous princes and nobles as their attendants; so here. The services of God's attendants are reverential, alert, individual, harmonious, enthusiastic.
4. *His absolute holiness*—HOLY! HOLY! HOLY!

II. HUMILIATION—SELF ABNEGATION
"Woe is me."
1. A deep sense of his personality—"I am undone." He feels himself singled out from the millions.
2. A sense of personal ruin.
3. A sense of personal sin.
4. A sense of the true condition of others.

III. PURIFICATION
"Then flew one of the seraphims, etc."
1. Thine iniquity is taken away; taken by another and at what a cost! "The Lord hath laid on him the iniquity of us all."
2. Thy sin purged;—The Holy Spirit, like fire, purifies, melts, refines, energizes.

IV. CONSECRATION
"Here am I."
1. The King is not in straits for servants to carry His message.
2. Neither is He ignorant as to who will answer the call.
3. When men are divinely prepared, they will respond. "Here am I, etc."
Sin has injured man's capacity for seeing God.
The Gospel restores this capacity—opens the spiritual eyes, etc.

Where? What?

Mrs. Gordon Wishart, Class of '26, Toronto, Canada

"Where are you? What are you doing?" These are some of the questions which "backed" the lovely Christmas cards received from old friends with whom this annual extending of the Season's Greetings is the only contact. Yes, and they are the very questions which arise at the mention of some of your names, or the thoughts of you which often steal across the plain of years. Then too, some of you, almost forgotten, will unexpectedly invade the realm of sleep, and after seeing you in our dreams, we awaken to ask, "Where are they? What are they doing?" Occasionally we have the joy of meeting some one who knows the answers as far as some are concerned, but in the majority of cases the questions remain unanswered.

What is the very first page to which you turn upon receipt of your copy of The Vision? Be honest now. Do you drink in the splendid editorials, peruse thoughtfully the excellent expositions, and then several days after having received your copy do you finally find time for the page, "With The Fellowship Circle"? I must confess that I read the Vision as I would (if I could) read Hebrew or Chinese. I begin at the back and work forward. Why? Because I am seeking the answers to those popular questions, Where are you, and what are you doing?

Since human nature is much the same I took for granted that you would prefer my answer to those two questions to my attempting a wordy discourse, a homiletical review, or an exposition of some passage upon which you yourself could more ably "exposify." In fact, just two days after receiving Brother Witmer's request for this article, I had the long anticipated joy of spending a day with a good old B. T. S. pal. Upon informing her of the task assigned me, she very frankly replied, "For goodness sake, don't send in a sermon whatever you do. Just write something about yourself and your work and be sure and put some 'punch' into it." (End of quote)

Where are you? Well, we do have a home in Toronto, Ontario, but we are rarely there for we are constantly "going to and fro throughout the earth" (not seeking whom we may devour) but seeking to lead the lost to the Lord Jesus Christ.

What are you doing? For three years we pioneered in Western Canada where, though strenuous work and much sacrifice were involved, the results were most gratifying in that a flourishing Alliance church was established in Saskatchewan's capital city, Regina. From among the young people saved during those three years of foundation laying, twenty-two are now in active Christian service; while from among those saved since we left the work seven years ago, many more have responded to the call of the Lord and a large additional number are either in active Christian work or preparing for the same. How we do praise God for having given us a small part in the founding of that work.

During our third year in Regina, God blessed our home with a blue-eyed, dimpled darling whom He entrusted to our care for just four very brief but exquisitely happy months, and then He took her to Himself.
She budded on earth, our baby fair,
To bloom in the heavenly garden rare.
No sin, no sickness, no death are there,
She's safe in the heavenly Gardener's care.
After her home-going, my husband resigned from the church which by that time was well established, the pioneering days being over, and the rigid sacrifice at first entailed, no longer necessary. Although it was hard to leave our dear people, the work into which we had put our very lives, and the lonely little grave out on the prairie, Father said, "Go" and for the true Christian soldier there is no alternative.

As general evangelists of the Christian and Missionary Alliance for the United States and Canada, the next three years found us constantly engaged in evangelistic services from Coast to Coast and from our northernmost work in Edmonton, Alberta, down to the Gulf of Mexico.

The last appointment on our Western tour three and a half years ago was Vancouver B. C., where the District Superintendent had scheduled us to open the third largest city in the Dominion to our Alliance truth and testimony. This was to be done by a two-week evangelistic campaign to be held in a rented hall. As God graciously blessed that meeting, and as the Superintendent did not have a man to put into the field to carry on the work, and as it seemed wrong to do nothing to conserve the benefits of the campaign, we felt led to cancel some of our engagements and remain in Vancouver until the work was established. We anticipated a six months' stay at the very most, but God kept us there three years. My, how we do praise Him for those three years! After the second week of meetings the work became self-supporting, God sending in every penny for our heavy overhead as well as for all of our own personal needs. Praise His dear Name!

Again, the work was of a pioneering nature, and my what a challenge to our faith! We began a new Alliance work in a new place with just two reliable families as a foundation, but God worked mightily and brought into the work the very finest type of people. He saved a group of young people who soon became known throughout the city for their spiritual fervor and their exploits for God. God bless them! My own Sunday School class was begun with one girl, but it grew until we had thirty-eight choice young women. From the two faithful Alliance women who for years had prayed for our missionaries, there developed a large group of faithful women who banded themselves together to pray for the regions beyond. Most of these women had never before prayed in public, but as week by week they took definite missionary requests to the Throne of Grace, they soon developed into real prayer warriors.

After three years of rich blessing, when once more the days of material sacrifice

were over, and many of the problems connected with starting a new work had been solved; when it would have been delightful and comparatively easy to have remained to build upon the foundation laid, God spoke. Once more we were commanded to press onward and upward; once more Father told us that we had been in that mount long enough; and once more a time of farewell overtook us. Again the heart strings were wrenched and torn, and again my husband handed his resignation to a heartbroken board. However, our people knew that we would not leave them save at the bidding of the Lord, and so they became tearfully reconciled to God's will. God graciously answered prayer in the matter of a successor, raising up a very fine godly man to build upon that foundation in the laying of which He had privileged us to have a small part.

We do not feel that we returned to the evangelistic field for we never really left it. We were doing real Pauline evangelism out on the Coast. We have, however, returned to the itinerant ministry which we re-entered last fall. We were very busy in Eastern Canada and the Eastern States until Christmas, and after concluding this, our second Ohio campaign, we leave for the Pacific Northwest, where we are booked for a series of meetings taking us up to our summer schedule of camp meetings.

We do praise God that in every campaign He has been pleased to save the lost, restore the backsliding, and sanctify believers. We enter each campaign believing Him for "fruit that shall remain," and to bless the ends of the earth as a result of the meetings. Therefore we do praise Him that most of the converts have gone on with God and today are staunch soldiers of the cross while not a few have gone forth to the whitened harvest fields and are today serving Him in distant lands, still others of whom are in training for that great service.

The verse upon which we go forth is, "Thanks be unto God who always leads us forth to triumph with the Anointed One, and who diffuses by us (oh, the wonder of it!) the fragrance of the knowl-
(Continued on page 18)

In The World Today

THE CRYING NEED OF THE CHURCH

Clarence E. Macartney, D. D., in Christian Life and Faith has well said: "The crying need of the hour in the Protestant Church is a revival of faith in the pulpits of her churches and in the students in her theological seminaries. An analysis of the views held by a representative group of five hundred active ministers of the Presbyterian, Methodist, Baptist, Lutheran, Episcopalian, Congregational and Evangelical Churches, reveals the following saddening and alarming facts:

Unbelief of Ministers

Of the 500 ministers in active service who were interrogated, 13% reject the distinguished doctrine of the Christian Church, the Trinity; 48% reject the Scriptural account of the creation of the world by God; 33% no longer believe in the devil, whose works Christ said He came to destroy; 38% do not believe in special revelation; 43% reject the plenary inspiration of the Scriptures; 28% do not believe that the Old Testament prophets were so inspired as to be able to predict the future events; 55% do not believe that the Bible is wholly free from myth and legend; 19% reject the account of the Incarnation as related by St. Matthew and St. Luke, that our Lord was born of the Virgin Mary; 19% do not believe that Jesus is equal with God; 24% reject the Atonement of Christ on the Cross for the remission of sins; 12% reject the resurrection of Christ as related in the Gospels; 34% no longer believe in the future punishment of the finally impenitent; 33% do not believe in the resurrection of the body; 27% do not believe that our Lord will come again to judge the quick and the dead; 33% reject the fall of man from a state of original righteousness, as taught in the Old Testament and the New Testament; 51% regard the two Protestant sacraments, Baptism and the Lord's Supper, as non-essential; and 39% think that well disposed persons who love God and deal justly should be received into the Church regardless of their beliefs concerning the great doctrines of salvation.

Unbelief of Theological Students

This record of the ministers is bad enough. But more appalling is the record of the unbelief prevailing among 200 students of five representative theological seminaries of the Protestant Church in America. 35% reject the Trinity; 82% the devil; 79% special revelation; 91% plenary inspiration of the Scriptures; 66% prophecy, in the sense of prediction; 95% hold that the Bible is not free from myth or legend; 51% reject the Virgin Birth of our Lord; 37% do not believe that Jesus was equal with God; 61% do not believe in the Atonement on the Cross for the sins of the world; 31% do not believe in the resurrection of Jesus as related in the Gospels; 76% reject hell; 69% do not believe in the resurrection of man's body after death; 70% reject the Fall; 52% reject the Sacraments as non-essentials, and 85% of these theological students hold that persons well-disposed towards God and man should be taken into the Christian Church regardless of what they believe about Christ and the Way of Salvation."

"IT'S LATER THAN YOU THINK"

From a recent editorial of a daily paper we cull the following: "Hitler rules by the sword." Yes. But how long could he wield the sword if he did not also control his country's purse? By taxes, Hitler gathers into the public treasury 40% of Germany's total income. He personally controls two-thirds of this amount. Here in America, our governments (Federal, State and local) already collect from 25 to 30 per cent of the American income. And we have broken all American precedents by granting the President personal control over an enormous percentage of our total tax collections. In the words of a currently advertised book, "It's later than you think." But not too late if the people will keep reminding their representatives at Washington that they want no foreign entanglements, that they demand strict neutrality, that they want an end to star-chamber, tariff-slashing, that they want Congressional control over the national purse-strings. "It's later than you think." In the ninth consecutive year of deficits, the Federal budget is now com-

(Continued on page 18)

Flashes from the Mission Front

Appalling Need in Near East

The Near East takes in the countries that surround the Holy Land—the very ones in which Christianity once flourished. We need but reflect about the centers of the first years of the Christian era: Jerusalem, Antioch, Ephesus. The strongholds of the early church were in these cities. But today Mohammedanism covers the Near East like a blighting curse. The national churches are for the most part corrupt and formal; Judaism is bigoted and defiant.

The following facts given in World Dominion should make every reader pause for prayer that the Spirit of God might move among these lost millions. In Turkey, with a population of 16,158,018 there are only 1,847 Christians. Missionaries number 95 or 5 to the million. In Irak there are 349 Christians among the 2,857,077 people composing this kingdom. Missionaries number only 22. The population of Persia is given at 15,000,000 with 3,373 Christians. But the country that has fewest Christians is Arabia. In this vast desert peninsula with a population of seven million there are only 23 Christians. Missionary work has been carried on for many years by the Dutch Reformed Church of America and the Church of Scotland, but with very meager results. There are now 38 missionaries and 8 hospitals — almost 2 missionaries to every native Christian.

A New Survey

The International Missionary Council has just published an "interpretative Statistical Survey of the World Mission of the Christian Church." This work succeeds the splendid atlas and survey published in 1925 and is the most authoritative and comprehensive survey of missions in existence.

According to the new statistics missionaries—men and women, ordained and lay, doctors and teachers, married and unmarried—now number 27,483, for Asia, Africa, Latin America, and the Island World, as compared with 28,010 in 1925, a drop of 527 since the statistics of the World Missionary Atlas were gathered. This decrease appears surprisingly small in view

of the long-continued depression in so-called home-base lands and of the marked drop in income experienced by many boards. The number of foreign missionaries in Asia (including Turkey in Europe) decreased by 2,345, or from 16,663 to 14,318, during the period of thirteen years. Australasia, Netherlands, Indies and Oceania together have decreased by 43, or from 1,810 to 1,767, indicating no significant change in number for this general area. Missionaries in Latin America together with all the West Indies have decreased from 3,249 to 2,951, or by 298. Africa, on the other hand, shows the extraordinary increase in foreign staff from 6,289 to 8,447, or a gain of 2,158.

"In spite of the drop in total foreign staff, ordained missionaries have more than held their own, and in fact number 7,518 in 1938 as compared with 7,277 in 1925. In per cent of the total, ordained missionaries now comprise 27.35 per cent as compared with 24.55 per cent thirteen years ago. Men not ordained now number 3,427 as compared with 3,710 in 1925, a drop of 283. Short term workers of both sexes number 310 as compared with 382 in 1925—no hint here of any departure from full life service as the normal expectation in foreign appointments. Men doctors among the foreign staff have dropped in number from 781 to 619 since 1925; women doctors from 353 to 291; but foreign nurses have increased from 987 to 1,232, indicating a marked development in emphasis on the field of nursing and nurses' training.

"The total salaried staff of nationals, both men and women, connected with the missions and churches in the fields of missionary concern increased by a third from 1925 to 1938, or from 150,673 to 203,468. All the major areas show marked increases, but as in the case of foreign missionaries, Africa shows the greatest relative increase (84%) as compared, say, with that of Asia (1-3 per cent). But whereas both Africa and Asia have exhibited a fairly steady increase in national staff throughout the nineteenth century thus far, as shown by the four major statistical studies of the period, an extra-

(Continued on page 18)

With The Fellowship Circle

Lima, Peru, Jan. 4

"New Year's eve we met with God's children in the Mission Hall to spend the last hours of the old year in prayer, meditation and praise. God was with us in blessing. Our hearts were filled with praise and thanksgiving as one after another gave their testimony telling of the blessings and spiritual help received during the past year. One man said it had been his happiest year, as just a year ago he came to know the Lord as his Saviour. Another young man testified: 'Before I knew the Lord I worked in a liquor factory. After my conversion God showed me that I should not be in such a business as I was helping in the ruination of others. In answer to prayer God gave me a better business during this year and I have joy and peace in my heart serving the Lord.'

God met us in our time of prayer. We felt His presence in our midst. Our prayer has been that God would send us a gracious revival. We desire to see more souls saved than in previous years and we ask that you pray with us to this end."
—**Rev. C. D. Steiner.**

Malkapur, Jan. 4

"You will rejoice with us that four new converts were baptized last Sunday in this barren district. Others are interested. Please pray that they also will come wholeheartedly into the fold of Christ."—**Mrs. Tilman Amstutz.**

Siushan, Kweichow-Szechuan, Dec. 22

"The country north of us is in a very unsettled condition. Nearly a thousand brigands have virtually taken control of Lungtan and its vicinity. I felt led to go to Lungtan to visit and encourage our Chinese workers there. Although ordinarily it is not safe to travel overland, providentially I was able to travel with a fleet of trucks both going and returning. I found three of the main leaders living on the streets. There has been a lot of burglary, many of the country people had been robbed and some taken for ransom. Some, for fear of being taken, could not remain in their homes at night so stay somewhere on the mountainside or in some cave. A son of one of our Christians was one day taken off by two men to a side street and shot, yet for fear, little was said or done about this case. . . In spite of these conditions it was my happy opportunity to call on the main leader and witness to him of the saving grace of our Lord Jesus, leaving with him some good literature. He was very friendly and asked more about the Gospel. The Mission has been entered three times by night but the workers are pressing on." Let us be faithful in prayer for all our Chinese Christians.—**Rev. R. J. Birkey.**

Big Laurel, Ky.

Dear Friends:

"Blessed be the God and Father of our Lord Jesus Christ, who hath blessed us with all spiritual blessings in heavenly places in Christ." Ephesians 1:3.

Last Friday was the closing day for the county schools. It has been a part of our program to visit the schools once a week with a Bible study. At Big Laurel we presented awards to those who were able to quote the assigned memory work, and it was a joy to hear them recite them. The children have always looked forward to the day we would bring the organ and have "singin'," as they express it. In fact, if something caused us to postpone our day with them, the next morning they would meet us with, "Are you all comin' up to have singin' today?"

Next Monday, the Lord willing, we will open our first daily Vacation Bible School here at Big Laurel, so possibly in our next letter we may be able to give you some news concerning it. We covet your earnest prayers for this new undertaking.

We have at last taken advantage of, what seems to us, a grand opportunity to begin work in a much neglected field five miles farther "down creek." We are still holding our place at Big Laurel too, but our forces may be divided this summer until God sees fit to send other workers. We do desire that only His will may be done.

We have a number of calls for Bibles here and could also use more in our own meetings. If any of you have one or more

16

16

that you are not using, would you not like to share it with our people?

May God richly bless you, one and all.

Yours in His fellowship,

Luella Miller.

India

Akola Berar, India.

Dear Folks at Home:

At present I am in Anjangaon overseeing the building work in lifting the hollows out of the roof here. There came a heavy windstorm at the beginning of the rainy season, and the roof leaked terribly. The rafters and the ridge lumber got soaked and soft, and with a heavy wet tiling on the rafters there came billows into the roof. My job is to iron them out.

Fred Schelander was up in Nasik for a month working on the revision work of the New Testament. He had just returned from bringing the kiddies home from Ooty and he was very tired after three nights on the train. So he asked me to come along to his little camp at Tandalwadi just the other side of Akot. Edna and the elder Mr. Schelander were there already. There was a little camp meeting there for enquirers and those who showed interest in becoming Christians— entirely among the Mahar caste. He asked me to come on Wednesday and preach Wednesday night for them as he was so tired, and also to preach on Thursday morning and then for me to come on to my building supervision work on the bungalow. I did as he requested, and we had a fine time.

I will not make a long story of it here. Enough to say that the meetings lasted Wednesday night 8:30 to 12:30 and Thursday morning 9:00 till 11:00 when we left. And Fred tells me that after we were gone the meeting began in real earnest again and did not wind up till about three o'clock—no dinner or anything between. Six children were dedicated at the meeting and seven adults and young men were baptized. Praise the Lord! I wish I could have been there for the latter part of the meeting too, but I was sent to Anjangaon for building work really. The preaching part was a bit of a side course—enjoyed very much by me. Last year in this area there were eighty baptisms. All of these were as the climaxes of little local con-

ventions such as the one I witnessed in Tandalwadi. Almost all those who came are relatives of Christians. God is using Fred and Edna mightily in this district. May the fires of revival spread. — **Bert Eicher and Family.**

Illness

Ezra Rupp, who has been bedfast in the home of his brother in Doge City, Kans., for some time, was recently taken to the State Sanitarium in Norton. Mr. Rupp is well cared for and has been improving, for which we thank God.

Berne, Ind.

Mr. and Mrs. Ernest R. Zehr are rejoicing over the birth of a son, Paul Ernest, on January 26, 1939.

Woodburn, Ind.

Sharon Marcell Gerig was born to Rev. and Mrs. Clarence Gerig on February 4. Weight, eight and one-fourth pounds.

Tennessee

Dear Co-Workers in Christ:

We have been in Tennessee about three and one-half months now. How time does fly! Some have raised the question as to whether our location here is a "permanent" one for us. The only answer we can give is that our future is in God's hands, and we expect to stay here until He sends us elsewhere. So, pray that the Lord will continue to make His will plain.

The Lord has been working in our midst. About a month ago, He opened the way for us to start a Bible class for children, in a school in our own community. Fridays, at the close of school, we meet in the schoolhouse. In fact, the teacher is giving us the last one-half hour of school time for the class—from 2:30 to 3:00 P. M. The children are very much interested and look forward to the classes. Their faces light up as they see us coming. The children like to sing the gospel choruses. After brief opening exercises, we have the classes—the younger children in one group, and the older children in the other. The older class takes notes which we dictate, covering the main points of the lesson. They have a memory verse to learn each week. Our chief aim is to help the children to make a personal and def-

(Continued on page 18)

Our Alma Mater

VISITING SPEAKERS

We have had the privilege of having with us quite a number of visiting speakers during the past month. These include Rev. Jared Gerig, Rev. A. W. Tozer, pastor of the Chicago Alliance Tabernacle, Rev. N. C. Beskin, a converted Jewish Rabbi, Rev. Andrew Spoolstra, Rev. and Mrs. David Rupp, Dr. Homer C. Gettle, a Christian business man of Fort Wayne, Kenneth Geiger, Dr. Harold Mason, President of Huntington College, Rev. E. J. Bulgin, eminent evangelist from Long Beach, California, and Miss Marjorie Burt from the Bethany Orphanage, Bethany, Ky.

As we think back upon the messages of these ministers of the Gospel, we feel grateful to God for the heart searching, the inspiration and working of the Holy Spirit in our hearts as they spoke to us.

SENIOR OFFICERS

The officers of this year's senior class are: Roy Ramseyer, president, Dorothy Hesselbart, vice president, Jane Bedsworth, secretary, and Paul Rupp, treasurer. The class is composed of twenty-nine prospective graduates.

COMMENCEMENT SPEAKER

Dr. H. C. Morrison, President Emeritus of Asbury College, Editor of the "Pentecostal Herald," and well-known champion of the Christian faith, is to give the commencement address for the graduating class, May 26, 1939.

ANOTHER HIKE

A few days preceding Lincoln's birthday a group of about forty "inside" and "outside" students hiked down to the Lincoln Life Insurance building to visit the Lincoln Museum. We found the collection very interesting and instructive. We also found that our vigorous walk gave us exceedingly good appetites for the evening meal which awaited us upon our return.

FIRESIDE SERVICE IN BETHANY HALL

The reception room in Bethany Hall, enshrouded in white and cleverly decorated to remind one of the cold North was a suitable place for the girls' fireside meeting of February 4. "Missions in Alaska" was the theme of the evening program.

After a large group of girls had assembled and seated themselves in Eskimo fashion about the room which was dimly lighted by candle and fireplace, the meeting began with several group choruses led by Mildred Thom who was the presiding officer for the evening.

The devotions were in charge of Mable Woods who used Rom. 1:13-15 for her Scripture reading. We then listened to a duet—"Love Lifted Him to Calvary" by the Burr sisters.

Jean Riseborough gave us a splendid talk describing Alaska and Eskimo life, followed by an interesting account of missionary work in Alaska by Gabriele Martig.

Jane Bedsworth read a letter from Mr. and Mrs. Charles Hull who are doing radio work in Alaska. After listening to these instructive talks we felt in closer touch and deeper sympathy with the missionary efforts in Alaska.

The rest of the time was spent in listening to an account by Mrs. William Dillon of some of the experiences which she and her husband had while serving as evangelistic singers in England, Scotland and Wales. We thoroughly enjoyed looking at the scrapbook which Mrs. Dillon had made of the collection they had gathered as they traveled.

The 9:45 bell having rung, we scattered to our homes with the sense of having spent a very pleasant and profitable evening.

Mrs. B. F. Leightner, Mrs. C. A. Gerber and Ruth Gerber were our guests for the evening.

PRESIDENT RAMSEYER TO BE HONORED

Our President, Rev. J. E. Ramseyer, has been nominated by Olivet College, Olivet, Ill., to receive the honorary degree of Doctor of Divinity. The degree will be conferred during the commencement week in June. All who know our President feel that he is highly deserving of this special recognition and that in his humble spirit he will wear the title well.

Rev. and Mrs. Ramseyer have been in the South for the past weeks but are returning to Fort Wayne in the week following March 5th. They report much blessing in their itinerary.

LIQUIDATION OF DEBT ON BETHANY HALL

The Committee is not able to report as much progress as it would like in liquidating the debt. An appeal was made to the constituency of the school with a view of wiping out the debt completely by March 23rd, the 9th anniversary of the dedication of Bethany Hall. While some have given generously, yet the response has not been as great as we had hoped. About $1,000 is still needed. We are hoping and praying that in the time that yet remains the debt may be cleared. (Gifts are to be sent to the Treasurer of the Liquidating Fund, S. A. Witmer, Bible Institute, Fort Wayne, Ind.)

Liquidating Committee.

IN THE WORLD TODAY

(Continued from page 13)

pletely out of line. We are passing the buck to our children at the rate of six thousand dollars a minute, three hundred and sixty thousand dollars an hour, nearly nine thousand thousand dollars a day. "It's later than you think." But, thank God, it's still not too late.

FLASHES FROM THE MISSION FRONT

(Continued from page 14)

ordinary situation in Latin America (with all the West Indies) is to be noted. For this area the national staff total for 1903 was 6,000; for 1911, it was 6,199; for 1925, 6,094; but for 1938 it is shown to be 10,312. The near-paralysis in respect to providing national leaders, a condition which seemed to exist in this region for several decades, now appears to have passed, and with a slowly dropping foreign personnel, the load is being taken over by a rapidly increasing staff of nationals."

Missionaries on Major Fields

The newly published statistics by the International Missionary Council show the number of missionaries on the major area as follows:

Asia	14,318
Africa	8,447
Australia and Islands of the Pacific	1,767
Latin America	2,951

The most encouraging fact in the statistics of 1938 is the remarkable increase of native Christians. The increase by years for all of the above fields is as follows:

1903	1,214,797
1911	2,301,772
1925	3,565,443
1938	6,045,726

WITH THE FELLOWSHIP CIRCLE

(Continued from page 16)

inite decision for Christ. Pray that Satan will be defeated in this place, and many children saved.

The regular school visitation work continues. Most of the schools give us a hearty co-operation, and it is quite evident that the Holy Spirit is working in hearts. We have visited many schools in our own county, and some in Scott, an adjoining county. We reached one rural school, in a rather remote place, just as the children were having their noon hour. The teacher, an elderly man, came out to the car to welcome us. Since the children were eating lunch, we decided to eat ours. Just a little later we went in the schoolhouse, and the children took their seats. They were a little timid, but some took part in the singing of some choruses. After having prayer, an object lesson was given on "The Door of The Heart." Several children had tears in their eyes as they saw their need of Christ.

Yours, in the **Unchanging One,**
Marion and Emanuel Stauffer.

WHERE? WHAT?

(Continued from page 12)

edge of Him in every place." II Cor. 2: 14, Lit. Trans.

We covet the prayers of each member of our great Fellowship Circle in which we are deeply grateful to be a small link.

Mrs. Gordon Wishart,
25 Fulton Ave.,
Toronto, Ont., Canada.

The Old Hymns

There's lots of music in 'em—the hymns of long ago,
And when some grey-haired brother sings the ones I used to know
I sorter want to take a hand—I think of days gone by—
"On Jordan's stormy banks I stand and cast a wishful eye."

There's lots of music in 'em—those dear, sweet hymns of old
With visions bright of lands of light and shining streets of gold,
And I hear 'em ringing—singing where Memory dreaming stands,
"From Greenland's icy mountains to India's coral strands."

They seem to sing forever of holier, sweeter days,
Where the lilies of the love of God bloomed white in all the ways;
And I want to hear their music from the old time meetin's rise
Till "I can read my title clear to mansions in the skies."

We never needed singin' books in them old days—we knew
The words, the tunes of every one—the dear old hymnbook through!
We didn't have no trumpets then, no organs built for show,
We only sang to praise the Lord "from whom all blessings flow."

An' so I love the good old hymns; and when my time shall come—
Before the light has left me, and my singing lips are dumb—
If I can hear 'em sing them, I'll pass without a sigh
To "Canaan's fair and happy land where my possessions lie."

FRANK L. STANTON.

He, therefore, is the devout man, who lives no longer to his own will, or the way and spirit of the world, but to the sole will of God; who considers God in everything, who serves God in everything, who makes all the parts of his common life parts of piety, by doing everything in the Name of God, and under such rules as are conformable to His glory.—WILLIAM LAW.

WHERE IS HAPPINESS TO BE FOUND?

Not in infidelity. Voltaire was an infidel of the most pronounced type. He wrote:- "I wish I had never been born."

Not in pleasure. Byron lived a life of preasure if anyone did. He wrote:- "The worm, the canker, and the grief are mine alone."

Not in money. Gould, the American millionaire, had plenty of that. When dying, he said:- "I suppose I am the most miserable devil on earth."

Not in position and fame. Beaconsfield enjoyed more than his share of both. He wrote:- "Youth is a mistake, manhood a struggle, old age a regret."

One and all they confirm Solomon's verdict, "All is vanity and vexation of spirit." (Ecc. 2:17.)

Where Then Is It To Be Found?

Jesus said, "I will see you again, and your heart shall rejoice, and your joy no man taketh from you" (John 16:22). The answer is simple:-

IN CHRIST ALONE

Taste for yourself, and you will say:-
"Now, none but Christ can satisfy;
None other Name for me;
There's love, and life, and lasting joy,
Lord Jesus, found in Thee."

F. H. B.

TWO SPECIAL EVENTS IN MARCH

DEDICATORY CONCERT—MARCH 14TH

The organ which was recently secured for the Bible Institute will be dedicated at a special concert on Tuesday evening, March 14th. An hour of sacred music featuring the playing of the Orgatron by Professor Weaver has been arranged. Mr. Weaver will be assisted by Mr. Gerig, pianist, Mr. Alfred Zahlout, violinist, and Mr. Richard Holzworth, soloist. The concert will be given in the First Missionary Church at 8:00 o'clock. The public is cordially invited and a special invitation is given to members of the Fellowship Circle—which is undertaking to give some assistance toward the purchase of the instrument.

*

35TH ANNIVERSARY SERVICE – MARCH 21ST

One week later, on the evening of March 21st, another event will take place which will be of interest to all former students and the many friends of the Institute. The 35th anniversary of the founding of the Institute will be commemorated. 35 years ago the main building was completed and classes begun in Fort Wayne, and nine years ago Bethany Hall was built.

The work of three men whose lives were given to the work of the Institute will be memorialized:

Rev. D. Y. Schultz, Cofounder and Superintendent—1904-1911

Rev. B. P. Lugibihl, Cofounder and Business Manager—1904-1916

Rev. Byron G. Smith, Instructor—1925-1934

All friends and former students of the Institute are invited to attend. The Board of Trustees will be in session on that day and will be in attendance. A great service is anticipated which we trust will mark a milestone in the history of the school.

CPSIA information can be obtained
at www.ICGtesting.com
Printed in the USA
LVHW081448211118
597922LV00010B/643/P